CosiCosa is an organization created by Cristina Valero, Laura Malinverni, Isabel Garcia, and Marie-Monique Schaper in 2018. Its objective is to create activities and experiences that will help children to develop their creative and social skills and improve their self-knowledge through new technologies, and to help build on critical thinking and reflection to confront future ethical issues that are brought by emerging new technologies.

CosiCosa has collaborated with schools, libraries, and other educational institutions to educate in subjects like the ethical dilemmas of artificial intelligence, gender representation, privacy, and its impact in our capacities. It was awarded the 2018 Mobile Week Gallery prize, the 2018 Cotec Innovation prize, 2019 Educational Innovation prize, and 2020's Barcelona grants.

cosicosa.tech

Ana Seixas is a Portuguese illustrator and graphic designer. She studied design in Aveiro's university and in the BAU Design College of Barcelona. It was there where she discovered the illustration world and continued her studies in this discipline in the EINA University School of Design and Art of Barcelona.

Once, she was asked how she would illustrate her life and she answered she'd draw a circus filled with tightrope walkers and jugglers working together to keep everything in balance. Since 2008, Seixas combines her work with illustrations of magazines, publicity campaigns, packaging, and books with her own projects of engraving and ceramics.

She's currently working in Porto, where she lives with her two cats.

anaseixas.com

Hello, Robot!

Illustrated by Ana Seixas
Written by CosiCosa

Translation from Spanish by Rosa Gomez
Font: Fairplex Narrow OT by Zuzana Licko, Neusa Next by Mariya V. Pigoulevskaya, Nexa Rust Sans by Fontfabric, Palmer Lake by Jen Wagner Co.

Printed by Schleunungdruck GmbH, Marktheidenfeld
Made in Germany

Published by Little Gestalten, Berlin 2022
ISBN 978-3-96704-735-6

The Spanish original edition *Entre máquinas inteligentes* was published by Editorial Flamboyant S.L.
www.editorialflamboyant.com

©Editorial Flamboyant S.L., 2022
©Illustrations: Ana Seixas, 2021
©Texts and script: CosiCosa, 2021
©for the English edition: Little Gestalten, an imprint of Die Gestalten Verlag GmbH & Co. KG, Berlin 2022.

All rights reserved. No part of this publication may be reproduced or transmitted in any form or by any means, electronic or mechanical, including photocopy or any storage and retrieval system, without permission in writing from the publisher.

Respect copyrights, encourage creativity!

For more information, and to order books, please visit www.little.gestalten.com.

Bibliographic information published by the Deutsche Nationalbibliothek.
The Deutsche Nationalbibliothek lists this publication in the Deutsche Nationalbibliografie; detailed bibliographic data are available online at www.dnb.de.

This book was printed on paper certified according to the standards of the FSC®.

HELLO, ROBOT!
DAY-TO-DAY LIFE WITH ARTIFICIAL INTELLIGENCE

COSICOSA · ANA SEIXAS

CONTENTS

Timeline 08
Smart Machines 14
Can We Know if a Machine is Smart?......................16
Machines That Learn 20
Coding the Perfect Recipe 26
Friends Without Flesh and Blood 34
Who Is Listening?..38
Can They Understand How We Feel?......................40
What Do You Recommend? 45
The Filter Bubble 48
Replaced by Machines?..50
I Am a Machine! 54
Daily Smart Technologies 58
How Addictive! 64
Who Changes Who? 66
Imagine the Future! 67
Glossary 68
Bibliography and References 69

Could we consider this boat as one of the first imagined ancestors of self-driving cars?

In Greek mythology, the boat that book Ulysses back to Ithaca sailed autonomously, commanded only by thoughts.

280-220 CE

Philo of Byzantium invented the automatic server—an automaton that filled a cup when placed into its hand.

1495

Leonardo Da Vinci designed a robotic knight. According to his plans, it would be able to make several movements, such as sitting, and moving its arms, neck, and jaw. We don't know if he ever tried to build it, but the constructions made from his designs in modern times were fully functional.

CIRCA 1200

It's believed that Albertus Magnus built a robotic head that was able to guard his doors and welcome his guests.

1612

In the book, *Don Quixote,* we can read the curious story of Don Quixote's encounter with a talking bronze bust that can answer all kinds of questions.

Legend says that when his daughter died, French philosopher Rene Descartes built an automaton to look just like her. When the sailors transporting the automaton saw it for the first time, they got scared and threw her into the sea.

Did the idea of a talking head that knows the answer to any question help us come up with the idea to build the digital assistants we use today?

"TO WITHDRAW IS NOT TO RUN AWAY"

1646

1738

Jacques de Vaucanson built a robotic duck that was able to eat, digest the food, and relieve itself. This duck is considered the **first robotic pet** in history.

1783

Wolfgang von Kempelen created a **chess playing machine** for the Austrian

1942

In the short story *Runaround*, Isaac Asimov devises the three **laws of robotics**.

1st law: A robot may not injure a human being or, through inaction, allow a human being to come to harm.

2nd law: A robot must obey the orders given to it by human beings, except where such orders would conflict with the first law.

3rd law: A robot must protect its own existence as long as such protection does not conflict with the first or second law.

1920

In the play *R.U.R.*, the writer Karel Čapek tells the story of a man who **builds robots to reduce the people's workload.** Even though they are created to help humanity, they end up starting a revolution that will destroy it.

1947

2016

The artist Pinar Yoldas created the project, *Kitty AI: Artificial Intelligence for Governance,* where she imagines a world set in the year 2039, in which **artificial intelligence** takes over politics and an AI kitten becomes the first **non-human governor.**

Queen Maria Theresia... Or at least, that's what he made everyone believe! Actually, there was an expert chess player hidden inside the machine, moving the pieces.

Many years later in 1996, IBM built the supercomputer Deepblue that was able to win over the ranking world chess champion.

1817

In the short story, *The Sandman,* by E.T.A. Hoffmann, a young student falls in love with Olympia without knowing that she's an automaton. A similar idea is shown in the movie *Her,* by Spike Jonze (2013), in which the main character **falls in love with his phone's voice assistant.**

Do you think it's possible to fall in love with a robot?

1899

In *In the Year 2889,* Jules Verne describes the **phonotelephote**—a system that allowed the transmission of images through a series of mirrors connected by cables.

In the novel *With Folded Hands,* writer Jack Williamson describes a world in which robots are so effective that humans have nothing to do.

This idea is also shown in the movie *Wall-e,* by Andrew Stanton (2008). In it, **intelligent technology deals with every human task** and human beings have nothing to do but sit and watch their screens.

IMPORTANT

All fiction stories about intelligent technology are fundamental in the development of our fears and hopes on them.

2015

In the movie *Avengers: Age of Ultron,* by Joss Whedon, a group of superheroes fight against an artificial intelligence. Even though it was created to protect humanity, it has decided that the **main threat is humanity** itself and wants to annihilate them.

1999

The movie *Bicentennial Man* is the story of a **robot who learns how to think and feel,** and chooses to become a human being with all its advantages—and inconveniences.

11

SMART MACHINES

The basic objective of artificial intelligence is to do the same things that our human minds can do. For example, problem solving, communicating with others, making decisions, planning, give orders to move around…

Can a Smart computer do all of those things? What about a Smart vacuum? OK, maybe it can't do every single one of those things, but they can do some of them, and that's why we always add the adjective *Smart* when we are talking about these kinds of objects.

Throughout this book, we are going to question a lot of things about Smart machines, starting with the question, 'Are they really smart?'. We'll see how they work, how they impact our lives, and the ethical issues that they bring up.

Shall we begin?

Ada Lovelace has been recognised as the first programmer in history—she believed that **machines can't be intelligent by themselves because they only do what they are programmed to do.**

Is a machine's intelligence the same as a person's?

Can a machine be as intelligent as a person?

What about more intelligent than a dog?

IMPORTANT

Smart technology has only been programmed to perform specific tasks. They can't do everything!

CAN WE KNOW IF A MACHINE IS SMART?

You are not the first person to ask this question. In 1950, the mathematician **Alan Turing** designed a test to evaluate whether or not a machine can be as intelligent as a human being. The test involves asking the same questions to two subjects (a computer and a person) separately. If when analyzing the answers of both subjects, the person tasked with marking the test is incapable of differentiating who had answered each question, the machine passes the **Turing Test** and is considered intelligent.

But Turing's test was not infallible. As a matter of fact, the philosopher **John Searle** thought of a mental experiment to criticize Turing's test called **The Chinese Room.** Let's imagine that we build a machine that can understand and speak Chinese. We perform the Turing test, that is, the machine receives Chinese phrases from a person and answers coherently. So, the person would believe that whoever is answering the questions understands Chinese, therefore, the machine passes the test.

But does it really understand Chinese?

Now, let's imagine that this is not a machine, but John Searle pretending to be a machine (or is him hidden inside of it!). He doesn't know a single word of Chinese, but he has books and manuals telling him the rules to follow (For example, if you receive these bunch of symbols, answer with these other ones). Following these instructions, Searle would be able to answer any question—all without understanding a single word!

TRUE OR FALSE?

1 IN AN EXPERIMENT AT A LONDON UNIVERSITY, THE PARTICIPANTS DIDN'T NOTICE THAT ONE OF THE 'STUDENTS' WAS A ROBOT.

2 IN A SWISS UNIVERSITY, A GROUP OF ROBOTS PROGRAMMED TO COOPERATE ENDED UP LEARNING HOW TO LIE TO EACH OTHER.

3 IN THE USA, A FLYING ROBOT WAS DEVELOPED THAT LOOKED, AND MOVED SO MUCH LIKE A REAL BIRD THAT IT WAS ATTACKED BY A FALCON.

4 DURING A WAR, A ROBOT HAD TO BE DESTORYED BECAUSE IT DECIDED—BY ITSELF—TO SWITCH SIDES.

ANSWERS: 1) False, 2) True, 3) True, 4) False

DOUBTS DOUBTS DOUBTS

HMMM...

How would you work out if a machine is smart?

HELLO!

Did you know your neighbour is a robot? What do you mean they're not? Prove it!

WHO IS IT?

If someone calls you, can you be 100 percent sure they're not a machine?

19

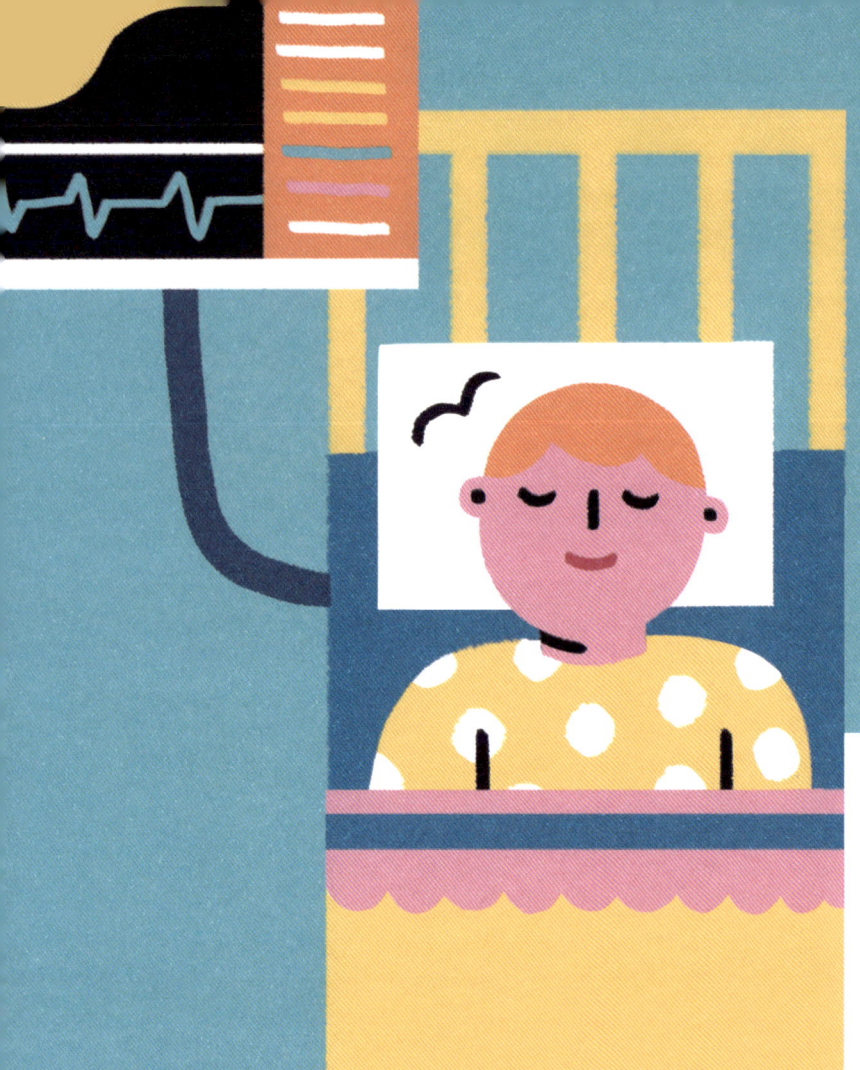

SMART MACHINES ARE CAPABLE OF **MAKING PREDICTIONS ABOUT THE EVOLUTION AND TREATMENT OF PATIENTS.**

They receive and analyze patient diagnostic data, treatment, and evolution. From that data, they look for common patterns and generate predictions on the evolution of other patients.

MACHINES THAT LEARN

SMART MACHINES CAN **RECOMMEND MUSIC OR VIDEOS THAT YOU MIGHT ENJOY.**

They analyze the data that the system has about you (listening habits, taste preference, etc.), look for other users that have made similar decisions, and generate personalized recommendations.

SMART MACHINES THAT CAN PERFORM HOUSEWORK, LIKE SWEEPING OR CLEANING, AUTONOMOUSLY.

Using their surroundings data (obstacles, changes of level, dirt ...) obtained through sensors. With the collected information, they decide what should their behaviour be.

Nowadays, a technology is considered Smart when it can do a task autonomously. For example, making predictions, giving recommendations, or making decisions. For this to be possible, programmes are created that allow the machine to learn from the data received.

How do they learn? They analyze a large quantity of data, from which **they'll find patterns**—models used to recognize other things that are equal or similar.

SMART MACHINES THAT CAN RECOGNIZE HUMAN FACES.

They receive a great number of images of faces, then from those, they create patterns that allow them to know what is a face and what is not.

DO THEY LEARN THE SAME WAY WE DO?

Have you ever wondered how a baby learns to recognize a dog?

There's a lot we don't yet know about how we learn, although there are different theories. Artificial intelligence designers use these theories to program the machines' learning skills.

YOU ARE NOT A DOG

YES, I AM A DOG!

Imagine a machine that has been trained to recognise dogs only from pictures of Dalmatians. It would be incapable of considering a Bulldog or a Husky a dog. Even though Dalmatians are dogs, they do not represent every kind of dog.

Smart machines need to receive a large amount of data (facts, numbers, images, sounds, or any other kind of information) to build predictions, make models and make the right choices. For example, for our machine to be able to recognize dogs, it would need a lot of images of every kind of dog. That way, it could differentiate between the characteristics that make dogs different than any other kind of animals (and any other kind of objects or things).

IMAGINE WHAT WOULD HAPPEN IF...

...AN ALIEN CAME TO EARTH AND SAW ONLY CHILDREN?

...THERE WAS A SYSTEM TO RECOGNIZE PEOPLE ONLY SAW IMAGES OF BLONDE PEOPLE?

...THERE WAS A SYSTEM THAT DETERMINED IF SOMEONE WAS A GOOD OR BAD TEACHER USING ONLY THE STUDENTS SCORES AS DATA?

TRUE OR FALSE?

1 IN 2017, A COMPANY HAD TO STOP USING THEIR PERSONAL SELECTION ARTIFICIAL INTELLIGENCE PROGRAMME BECAUSE IT DISCRIMINATED AGAINST FEMALE APPLICANTS.

2 IN A RESTAURANT, A ROBOT IN CHARGE OF CLEANING TABLES MISTAKENLY THREW AWAY A CHILDREN'S TOY, THINKING IT WAS LEFTOVER FOOD!

3 DURING A FOOTBALL MATCH, THE ARTIFICIAL INTELLIGENCE TRANSMISSION SYSTEM MISTOOK A BALD REFEREE FOR THE BALL.

ANSWERS: 1) Truth; 2) False; 3) Truth

Every participant specified their favourite dishes' ingredients and has given the preparation instructions. With this information, the robot generated a unique recipe.

Do you think the machine has been able to make the perfect meal?

Would you eat it?

As there was not one single idea of what perfect food is, the results are a mess!

Smart machines are designed and programmed by people that decide what information is important for the system to execute its tasks. Here, in the case of the perfect food, every person has their own beliefs and opinions, and this may be reflected in the data selection (the ingredients) and the machine programming (the instructions).

Can a machine please everyone?

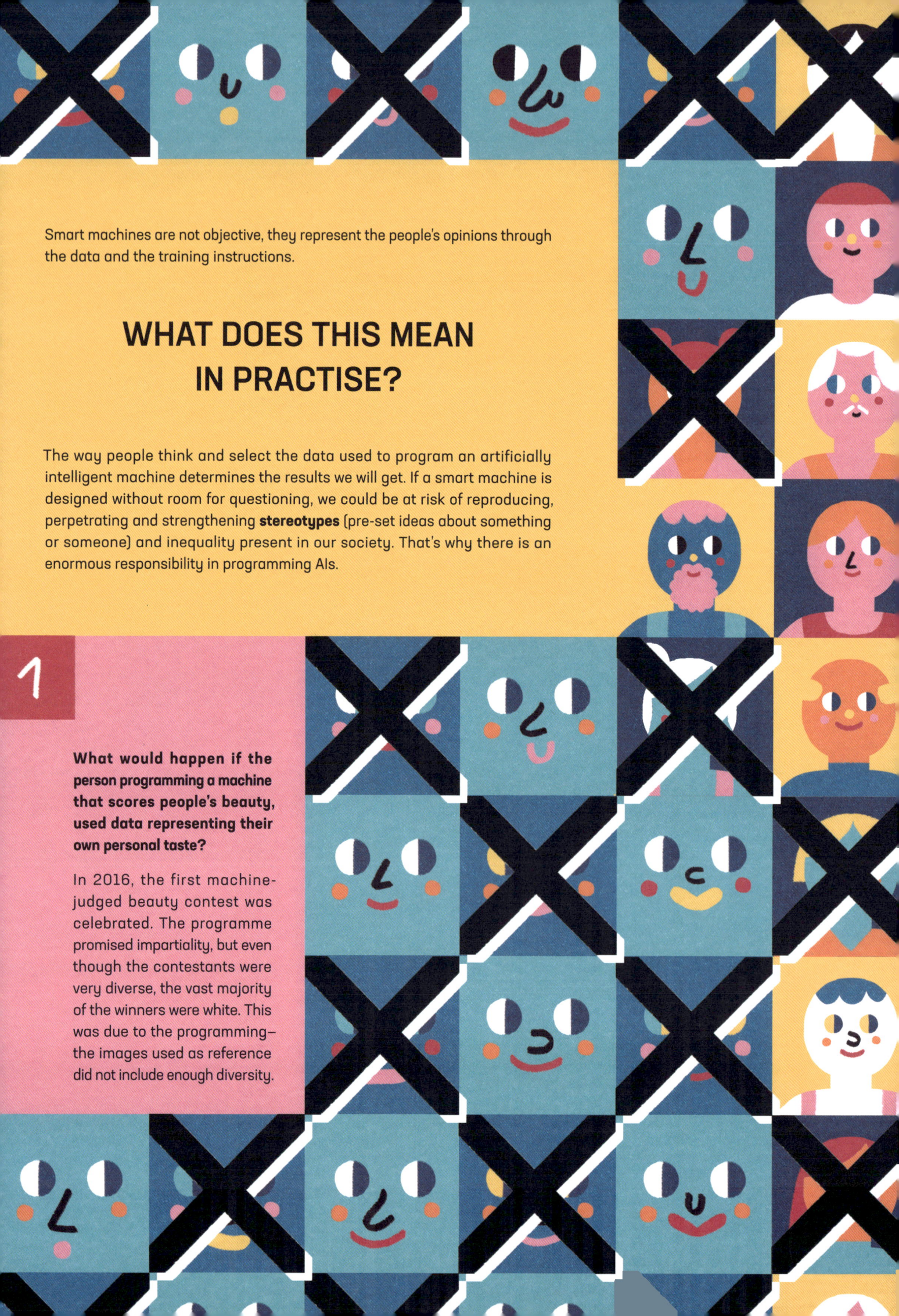

Smart machines are not objective, they represent the people's opinions through the data and the training instructions.

WHAT DOES THIS MEAN IN PRACTISE?

The way people think and select the data used to program an artificially intelligent machine determines the results we will get. If a smart machine is designed without room for questioning, we could be at risk of reproducing, perpetrating and strengthening **stereotypes** (pre-set ideas about something or someone) and inequality present in our society. That's why there is an enormous responsibility in programming AIs.

1

What would happen if the person programming a machine that scores people's beauty, used data representing their own personal taste?

In 2016, the first machine-judged beauty contest was celebrated. The programme promised impartiality, but even though the contestants were very diverse, the vast majority of the winners were white. This was due to the programming—the images used as reference did not include enough diversity.

2

What would happen if we used the data from the last two hundred years to program a machine to determinate the necessary characteristics for someone to be a good scientist?

For a long-time, women had significantly less opportunities to work in the scientific fields and, in some cases, the ones that did make it had to present their work under a male pseudonym. If we only used this historical data as a reference, we run the risk of continuing to discriminate against women, since being a woman would not show up as a recurring characteristic for people who excel in science.

3

What would happen if someone decided that a criterion to judge whether or not you could trust a person was where they live?

If a bank used a smart programme to decide whether or not to loan money to people, and a person's zip code or post code was all the information they had available, people who lived in 'poorer' or seemingly 'less-desirable' areas may have less chance to be approved for a loan.

HOW DO YOU IMAGINE THESE PEOPLE?

Do you think you have decided because of stereotypes?

Often, without even realizing it, we judge other people based only on stereotypes: Intelligent people wear glasses, people that play basketball are tall, grandmothers are sweet and kind... Those preconceived notions can be reflected in the smart machine programming.

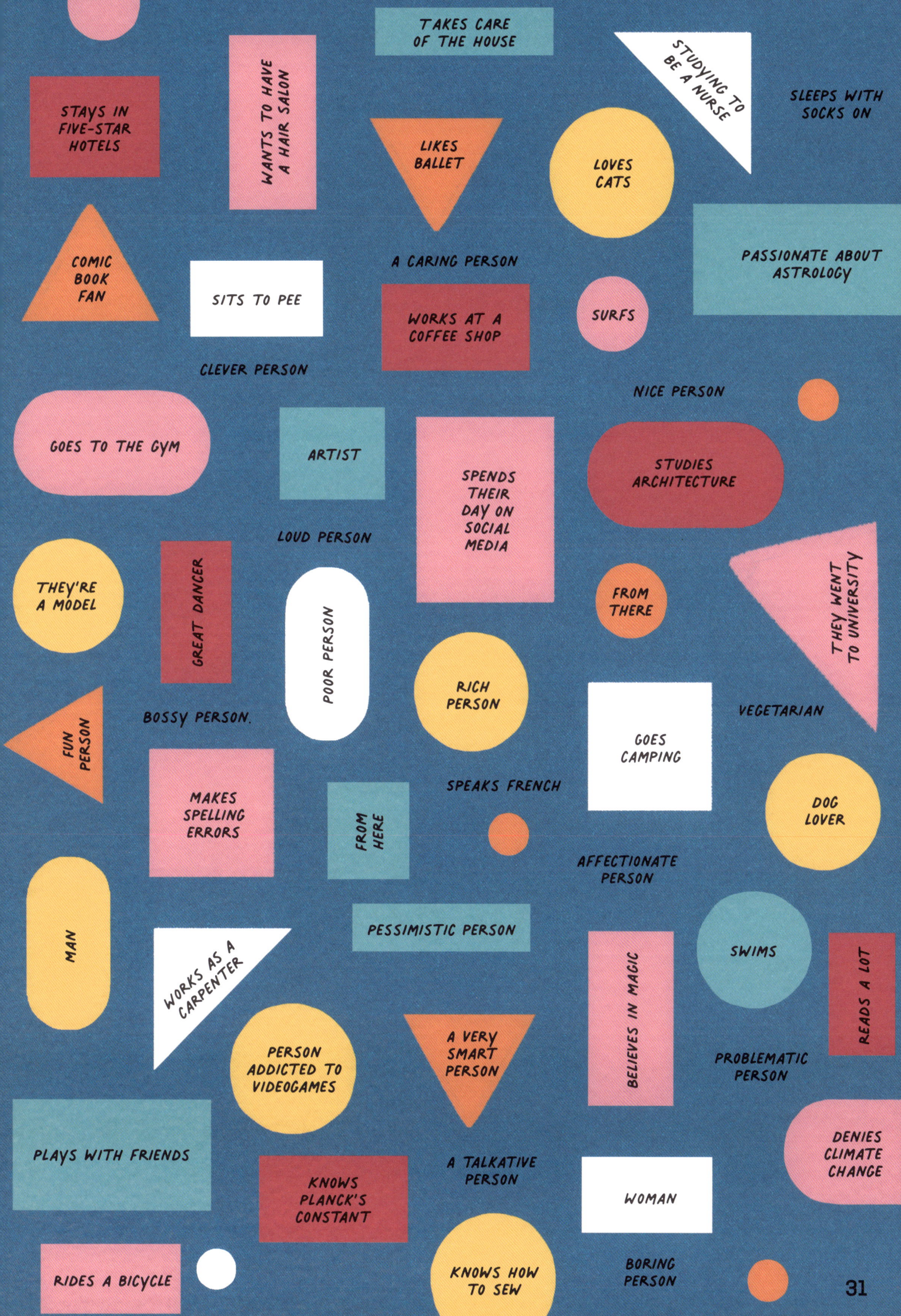

HAVE MORE DIVERSITY IN THE TEAMS THAT DESIGN SMART TECHNOLOGY.

SMART MACHINES WILL BE HOW WE WANT THEM TO BE.

INCLUDING SOCIAL SCIENCE AND ETHICS IN TECHNOLOGY COURSES.

SOCIOLOGY · PSYCHOLOGY · ANTHROPOLOGY · ETHICS

What can be done to reduce the risk of reproducing stereotypes and inequality?

ALLOWING PEOPLE WITH VERY DIFFERENT BACKGROUNDS TO REVIEW HOW SMART TECHNOLOGY WORKS.

CAN YOU THINK OF ANOTHER WAY?

Imagine that the roles need to cast be for the end of year play. If you had to program a machine to do it, what kind of data would you provide? How would you make sure that the right decisions are made?

FRIENDS WITHOUT FLESH AND BLOOD

WHY DO YOU THINK SOME PEOPLE HIDE FROM DIGITAL VOICE ASSISTANTS?

WOULD YOU TELL THE SAME THINGS TO A VOICE ASSISTANT THAN YOU WOULD TO A FRIEND OR YOUR PARENT?

— Can I tell you a secret?

— Yes, but let's go to my secret hiding place or Alexa will hear us.

In fairy tales, cartoons, and movies, there have always been animated objects that can talk and communicate with people. But nowadays it's not only in fiction—every day there are more objects around us that understand what we say and are able to talk and communicate with us.

HELLO!

OF COURSE!

Maybe the idea of **voice assistants** seems like a new one, but legend says that in the year 1200, philosopher Roger Bacon built a brass head capable of answering all questions...

WHAT CAN I HELP YOU WITH?

What do you think is the difference between the speaking objects from stories and the smart objects that communicate with us?

VROOOM...

HOW LONG UNTIL...?

Where did you put the shoes Nana gave me?

Where did you put the shoes Nana gave me?

35

Voice assistants are designed to recognize what we say and imitate the human voice. To do this, they need to receive data—that means voices and conversations. **They need to hear us!** If they didn't, they would not be able to communicate with people.

Even though machines can recognize conversations, it does not mean they understand them the way that people do.

1773

The doctor, physicist, and engineer Christian Kratzenstein was able **to reproduce vowels sounds** using resonant tubes connected to organ tubes.

1932

The Voder is invented, the first mechanism capable of **imitating speech.** It was not an autonomous machine—a person decided what sounds came out of it using a keyboard and a pedal.

VOICE RECOGNITION: A BRIEF CHRONOLOGY

To develop the voice recognition that we have nowadays, there has been centuries of studies and investigation.

THE 80s

Investigations were advancing—IBM designed Tangora, a technology able to **recognise 20,000 words.**

THE 90s

We can see in the market the first voice recognition programmes. For example, the dictation programme Dragon, able to **type out what someone had said aloud.**

1952

Audrey is designed, a machine capable of **recognizing numbers from zero to nine** when spoken by its creators. It measured more than two metres (six and a half feet) high and consumed a lot of energy.

2011

Siri is invented, an artificial intelligence with **personal assistant skills.**

WHO IS LISTENING?

Behind smart machines there is always a business or team developing its decision-making system. There are also other businesses interested in knowing, controlling, and using all the information that these machines can collect.

Personal data is a very valuable asset! It can be bought and sold. It provides the possibility of generating personalized content and publicity, and thanks to that, increase the selling chances of certain products or new services.

Knowing who is listening to us is getting harder every day.

Can we get out of the hiding place?

Of course, Alexa's battery died.

In the US, **98 percent of children** up to 11 years of age interact with voice assistants like Alexa. We are so used to asking questions that will be answered immediately by a voice assistant that we might eventually fall under the impression that everything can be done instantly! In a similar way, if we only play with smart toys that always agree with us, we might eventually want to avoid playing with people that do not share our opinions.

Have you also noticed that voice assistants usually have a feminine voice and are always kind and servile? Why do you think they're designed that way?

I DON'T WANT TO PLAY TODAY!

What would you do if a smart toy suddenly became unpleasant?

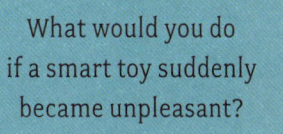

Would you change the way you play if you knew that there is a toy that records everything you say?

I AM GOING TO TELL YOU...

SHHH...

An interactive doll capable of holding a conversation was invented in 2015. To develop its conversational skills, it recorded the conversations held with the children that played with it in the company's computers and sent a daily report of the children's activities to the parents. Some countries, like Germany, have banned selling this toy due to **privacy worries.**

Have you ever thought that what you tell a machine can be heard by another person?

What would you do if an intelligent machine had stored a very important secret of yours?

CAN THEY UNDERSTAND HOW WE FEEL?

In the same way that there are machines capable of recognizing speech, technology is being developed to identify human emotions.

Oh...What a pity! You don't like it. I was excited to get it for you!

How beautiful grandma! I love it!

Stop it...I know you don't. Your bracelet shows me.

No, really, I love it!

Between grandma and her granddaughter there is a conflict. The girl's bracelet interprets her disappointment with the gift, although she says the opposite. Who should grandma believe? The machine or her granddaughter? Can we absolutely guarantee that the machine is correctly interpreting the girl's feelings? **Is it possible for a machine to understand better out emotions than we do?**

Facial expressions are one of the first ways that people learn to recognize other people's feelings and intentions.

Even though they have a lot of information to drive conclusions in regards of feelings, machines are not infallible. But then again, neither are people!

Human emotions are very complex and every person feels and expresses their feelings in a different way. There are a lot of factors that might unsettle our reactions and make reading our feelings properly very difficult.

Let's find out what machines do to recognize our feelings in two simple steps.

1

Recognize that a face is a face (not a ball, a loaf of bread, or a lemon). This technology is very present nowadays—when social media suggests tagging someone, playing with picture filters on social media, going through the airport security control or even unlocking your phone.

2

Analyzing a series of elements (facial expression, warmth, gestures, speech, etc.) to estimate what is the specific emotion felt by someone else.

41

Emotion recognition is being used more every day to improve our interactions with the surrounding smart technologies and make some tasks easier, prevent accidents, or simply to give us comfort and make us happier.

Imagine this: You come home in a bad mood and, as soon as you are inside, your house knows how to recognize it and programs your chair to give you a relaxing massage while playing your favourite movie.

What would it look like to live in a world where technology always tries to make us happy?

Why and for whom would this information be useful?

In the United Arab Emirates, surveillance cameras that detect people's facial expression have been installed in public spaces. That way they can know the general population's mood.

Imagine your computer detects that your homework is too difficult or too easy and that it causes you frustration, then adapts it so you can stop feeling that way.

In the education technologies field, there are more and more technologies being used to recognize the students' feelings.

Is it good that technology sometimes allows us to avoid frustration?

How would you like to be able to know exactly what other people were feeling?

A Chinese high school became famous because they installed facial recognition cameras in their classes. Every thirty seconds, the cameras scanned the students faces and sent the information to a computer that classified their expressions in seven emotions (happy, sad, disappointed, bothered, frightened, surprised, and neutral) and measured their concentration level. With that data, every student received a score which was shown on a screen installed at the back of the room.

What positives and negatives can you see in constantly being under surveillance?

43

Emotion recognition technology can be beneficial. For example, it's starting to be applied in cars to detect if the driver is alert and minimize the accident risk, or in robots designed to assist people that can't communicate in a standard way (these systems are used to better understand their needs). But is it always good to have our emotions recognized by machines?

In the last few years there have been controversial cases in which this technology has been used to foresee, provoke, or manipulate emotions and favour corporations, governments, or individuals' interests with questionable objectives. This is one of the reasons why some people prefer to stay away from these kinds of technologies and preserve their privacy.

If a machine is influencing our decisions, are we still free?

There are studies that prove that when we decide to buy something, we are often thinking with our emotions. That's why emotion recognition is being investigated thoroughly by some companies, to better understand people's reactions to different products or ads.

But we must keep in mind the fact that facial recognition doesn't work in the same way for everyone. Depending on how a machine is programmed, it's actions can be very useful for some people and completely wrong (or even dangerous!) for others.

In her studies, computer expert and activist **Joy Buolamwini** found out that facial recognition doesn't work properly with dark skinned women. The algorithm was only able to recognize her once she wore a white mask!

WHAT DO YOU RECOMMEND?

Some machines recognize speech, others recognize emotions, and some machines can recognize our preferences and give us recommendations on music, films, friends, shopping and much more. How do they do it?

I am searching this to confuse Google so it doesn't know I'm a child.

Got it! See? Now I am only getting ads for dentures!

A lot of the technologies that surround us use **artificial intelligence generated algorithms** to predict people's preferences and taste. To do it, they collect information about our interactions: what have we looked for, what have we "liked," what are we watching, where we have been, who are we following on social media…From this information (again, data!) people are classified into profiles, separated in groups of similar characteristics (age, gender, interests, preferences…), and then they can predict our taste and possible interests.

45

WHAT HAPPENED IN LAST PAGES' ILLUSTRATIONS?
BEFORE THE KID TRICKS GOOGLE, THIS IS HER PROFILE:

BEFORE

DATA

LEARNING ALGORITHM
Data is processed to define the profile.

RESULTS

GIRL
12 YEARS OLD
VIDEOGAMES
SPORTY
POP MUSIC
ANIMALS

RECOMMENDATION

FOLLOW THIS WINDSURFER YOUTUBER

FOLLOW

AFTER TRICKING GOOGLE, HER PROFILE IS MODIFIED AND LOOKS LIKE THIS:

AFTER

DATA

↓

LEARNING ALGORITHM
Data is processed to define the profile.

↓

RESULTS

MAN
81 YEARS OLD
HEALTHCARE
BOARD GAMES
ORGANIZED TRIPS

↓

RECOMMENDATION

OFFER DENTURES

BUY

THE FILTER BUBBLE

It's very convenient to have things we might like recommended to us because it helps us navigate through a huge amount of information available on the internet. But what would happen if machines only offered us content that they know we will like and the selection of videos, publicity, news, and else is completely adjusted to our taste?

The cyberactivity activist **Eli Pariser** was the first one to talk about the risk of only receiving personalised information. To talk about it he made up the term "Filter Bubble," because once we are in a bubble, we are completely isolated from anything outside of it.

What would the world look like if people only got together with people with their same interests and taste?

When we only hear opinions we agree with, we are limiting our own thoughts and it becomes more difficult for us to learn new things. If we are too closed off from the world in our own bubble, we are missing the chance to open our mind to different points of view.

Diversity is necessary—it enriches us!

REPLACED BY MACHINES?

Throughout history, different technologies have changed the way we work, creating new professions and making others obsolete. When the printer was invented in 1440, for example, the job of the scribe disappeared. They oversaw copying the books by hand! But, at the same time, new professions linked to the printer were created, like typographical composition or large-scale distribution.

Nevertheless, when a machine has become capable of performing a task the same way or better than a person, humanity fears becoming obsolete or ending up being replaced by machines. Because what would be our role if intelligent technology could do every task currently done by a person?

Go clean your room!

Don't worry dad. I've trained Lil'robot to do it.

Should we regulate what activities robots can do?

Don't you have homework?

No, Mom. Lil'Robot did it for me.

In the 18th century, steam engines replaced a lot of manual jobs, changing the working world forever. That's why this time is called the **industrial revolution.** Working people found themselves with a worse quality of life due to the use of machines in industrialised jobs: The working hours were longer, there was less demand for workers and salaries were reduced. In response to this, a group of British artisans called *luddites* started a movement: they organized themselves to destroy the industrial machinery that took away their jobs and made their working and personal life worse. Finally, the military had to intervene to stop their actions.

Do you think that machines were to blame on the worsening of their quality of life?

Could a movement like the luddites against technology happen again?

What would the world look like if the luddites had won their revolution?

It's expected that by 2030, intelligent technology will replace 30 percent of current businesses. 375 million people would need to change their jobs, but 300 million new jobs linked to non-automatised tasks will be created.

If a robot is performing a task, can we say it's working? Should it be paid a salary?

Artificial intelligence is being used increasingly in the process of job search and personal selection.

There are hotel receptions in Japan hosted by human looking robots.

There are roboticized warehouses were robots move merchandising. The European Union has been contemplating the creation of new laws that will regulate how to introduce robots in business.

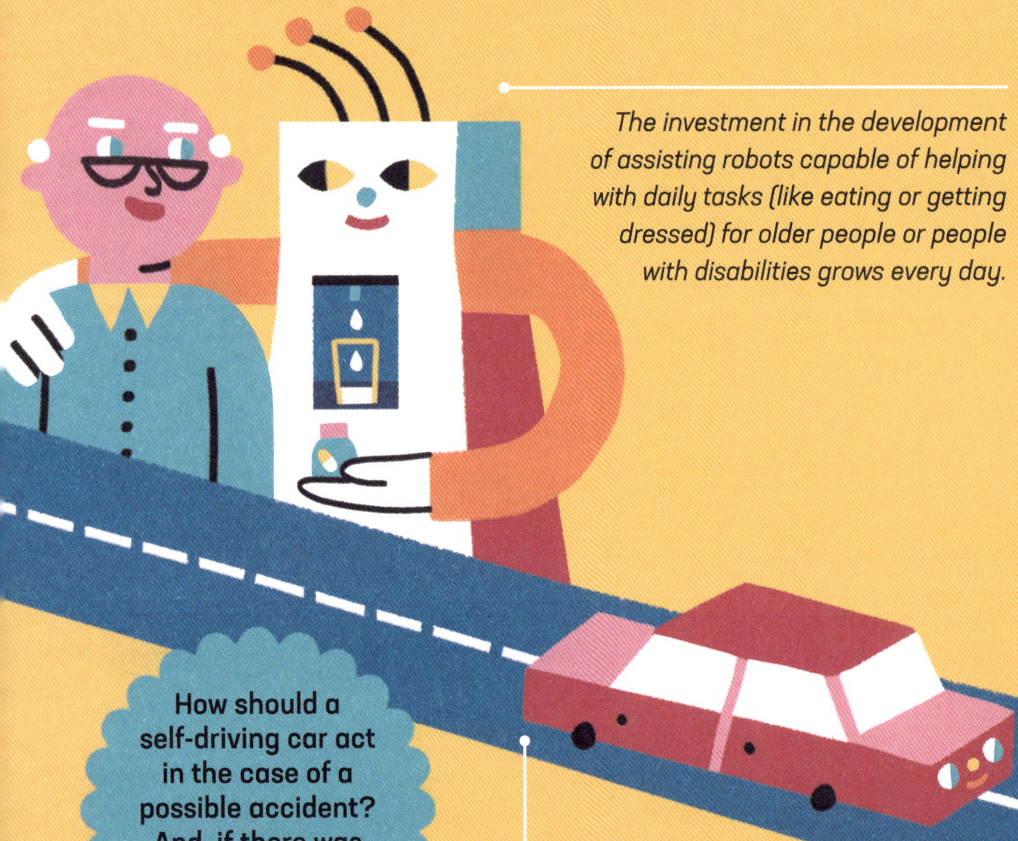

The investment in the development of assisting robots capable of helping with daily tasks (like eating or getting dressed) for older people or people with disabilities grows every day.

MORAL MACHINE

It's a platform that collects people's opinions on what choices a self-driving car should make in case of an accident. Answering the questions is not easy at all! For example, imagine that a self-driving car loses control and has two options: turn right and run over an old person with a dog or stay straight and run over a child.

What would you do?

How should a self-driving car act in the case of a possible accident? And, if there was an accident, whose fault would it be?

Autonomous cars, capable of imitating human driving abilities, already exist.

52

Our acceptance of the role that technology can have in our lives has changed through time. In 1800 luddites did not accept industrial machines, and nowadays, they form part of our everyday nature. What tasks are we open to trust to machines with? And which ones are we not able to trust them with? Do you think they'll be the same ones in the future?

Why don't you investigate a bit about it? Look for people of different ages and interview them. Here we can offer you some questions that can guide you, but you can make up way more! The answers could surprise you a lot!

INTERVIEW

- If you got sick, would you want to be taken care of by a machine?
- Would you like a smart machine to teach you a new language? Would you be a better or worse student?
- Would you trust a machine with the care of young children?
- Would you like to go to a robot dentist?
- Would you go to a restaurant where robots cook the food?
- Would you be uncomfortable if a machine advised you on who could be a good or bad friend?
- Would you be comfortable riding a self-driving bus?

I AM A MACHINE!

Lately, there has been a lot of investigation in smart prosthesis and implant development—technology capable of executing human bodily functions, resolving health issues, or improving our capacities. These prosthesis allow people that lost a body part like a leg or an arm, or that suffer other kind of issues, like diabetes, to replicate their previous activity.

This is not a new idea though; do you remember stories with pirates using hooks and peg legs? We have tried to resolve these issues for a long time with whatever we had available. But now, technological advances are allowing us to go even further.

Hugh Herr, also known as the *Bionic Man,* lost both legs in a terrible hiking accident. Not long after, he was again able to take part in his favourite sport thanks to intelligent prosthesis that, not only replicated the functionality of normal legs, but had characteristics that are non-existent in human beings, such as adjustable hight or titanium tips. These improvements made him an even more skilled hiker than he was before.

What's the difference between the bionic man and a pirate with a peg leg?

AT WHAT POINT DO WE BECOME CYBORGS?

A cyborg is a creature formed by living matter and electronic devices that improve their capacities. There are some very extreme cases of cyborgs, but it's not always that clear what could be counted as one. If a cyborg incorporates technological devices to increase their skills, then, can we say that if someone has always a telephone with them to remember phone numbers is also a cyborg? After all, it's a way to augment their skills and modify their behaviour!

GUESS: REALITY OR FICTION?

A — NEIL HARBISSON
Was born with achromatopsia, which means, he sees the world in a grey with no colours. That's why he got an antenna installed in his head that allows him to listen to colours through vibrations. He's able to differentiate between more than 300 colours—even infrareds and ultraviolets that are not perceivable by the human eye.

B — ROBOCOP
A police officer from Detroit, Alex James Murphy, better known as *RoboCop*, had armoured body parts and other technologies to increase his strength and perceptive abilities, with the objective to protect and serve the law in a more effective way.

C — ROB SPENCE
A filmmaker and lover of documentaries known as *Eyeborg*. He lost an eye when he was young and replaced it with a camera with which he recorded movies.

D — MOON RIBAS
This dancer implanted seismic sensors in her arm that to feel every earthquake on earth through vibrations on real rime. That way she can better feel the movements of the earth.

E — MOLLY MILLIONS
She works as a bodyguard. Among other things, she installed retracting blades in her nails through a precision surgery, so she always has a weapon on her. William Gibson made her the main character in some of his novels where Molly is a samurai cyborg.

F — INSPECTOR GADGET
The police inspector was famous for his bionic implants. The gadget ears, consisting of small cones that could be activated to hear better, his extendable arms, and the gadget phone, an implant in his hand!

Answers: Reality: A, C, D; Fiction: B, E, F.

THESEUS'S BOAT PARADOX

Theseus was the King and founder of Athens, on his way back to the Island of Crete with his crew in a very old and poorly maintained boat. During the journey, the crew did repaired he boat, replacing the broken pieces with others in better condition or recycling them to use them in different places of the boat.

When the boat finally got to port it had been completely modified. This posed the question, **was the boat in which Theseus came back the same one he left Crete on?**

If we are in a boat with thirty paddles and we exchange one paddle, is it still the same boat? What if we replace fifteen paddles? What if we also replaced the boat's structure? These questions become a paradox because it's very difficult to know exactly in which point replacing the parts of something makes it become a different thing. There are no right or wrong answers.

TURN RIGHT.

...you have a robotic eye on the back of your neck?

...you have a hearing aid?

WHAT DO YOU THINK?

It's very hard to know at what point do we become a hybrid with technology. Still, several contemporary thinkers believe that we are already cyborgs. Biologist and philosopher **Donna Haraway** defends that all of us are a product of hybridization between machines and organisms. Entrepreneur **Elon Musk** agrees, but in his case, he believes that we are cyborgs because we have a digital version in social media and we now have superpowers, like the ability to answer any question at any point, we can make videocalls with any person at any time and in any place, or send messages to millions of people instantly.

ARE YOU ALREADY A CYBORG IF...?

...you use the GPS to get to places?

HELLO!

...you have a hearing aid that allows you to understand every language in the world?

...you use your phone to remind you of what you must do?

...you have an electronic valve that helps you control the beating of your heart?

...you have a robotic leg?

Nowadays, technology already allows us to augment our capabilities. Do you think this makes the world more, or less fair?

DAILY SMART TECHNOLOGIES

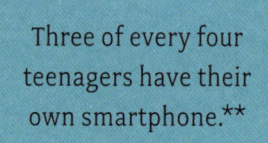

*2012 data from USA's Influence Central Agency
**2015 data from Spanish INE (Statistics National Institute)
***2021 data from AVACU (Valencian Users and Consumers Association)

42%
42 percent of children between five and seven have their own *tablet*.*

75%
Three of every four teenagers have their own smartphone.**

WHEN WERE SOME OF THE MOST USUAL TECHNOLOGIES POPULARISED?

In most cases between the creation of an invention and its daily use there are some years of investigation and tests. Inventions that today seem very extravagant can be as popular as television or smartphones by tomorrow!

TELEVISION

The first live show was transmitted in 1926, but it wasn't until the seventies when television became common in every home. Unlike today, there were very few channels, and they were in black and white.

COMPUTER

The first computer was invented in 1947, but we had to wait almost 40 years for it to become usable at home.

70%.

70 percent of young people between the ages of 12 and 15 have a social media profile.***

ATTENTION SPAN SHORTENING

According to a study done in 2000, people's attention span could be kept for 12 seconds. In 2015 it went down to eight seconds. This reduction of the attention span is attributed to the effects of an increasingly digital lifestyle.

INTERNET

The inventions that ended up creating the internet started in the seventies, but it was not until the beginning of the year 2000 that it became commonly used.

YOUTUBE

YouTube was created in 2005, the first entertainment platform that allowed you to share audio-visual content.

WHATSAPP

WhatsApp was created in 2009, originally it was a service in which you could recognize if someone could be called or receive a message. In 2010 it was used to send instant messages for the first time.

SMARTPHONE

The first smartphone was introduced in 1992. During the decade of 2010 it quickly became popular.

There are technologies that took a long time to become popular and others that we have assimilated to very quickly.

META

In 2021, Facebook became Meta, and started a transformation towards a new space to attempt to improve socialisation, learning, collaboration and play. The metaverse, in which virtual reality and augmented reality would be in the forefront.

PAINTING

TALKING WITH FRIENDS

READING

WATCHING CARTOONS

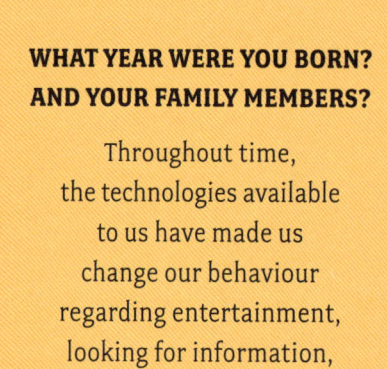

WHAT YEAR WERE YOU BORN? AND YOUR FAMILY MEMBERS?

Throughout time, the technologies available to us have made us change our behaviour regarding entertainment, looking for information, building relationships, etc.

LISTENING TO MUSIC

SAYING HI TO GRANDMA

PLAYING FOOTBALL

DOING HOMEWORK

LET'S INVESTIGATE!

CONDUCT LITTLE SURVEY WITH THE ADULTS CLOSE TO YOU TO DISCOVER HOW THINGS WERE DONE IN THEIR TIME.

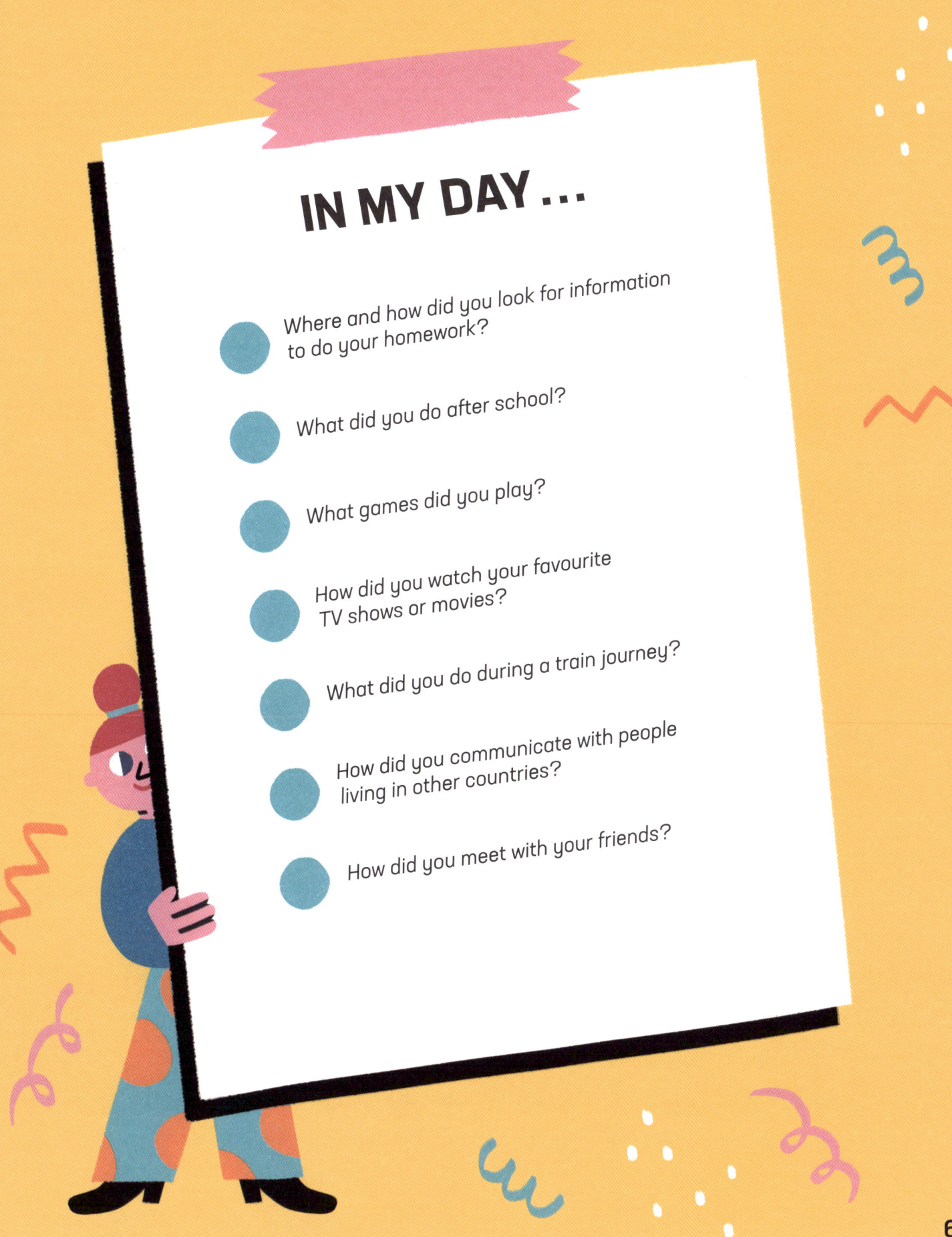

IN MY DAY …

- Where and how did you look for information to do your homework?
- What did you do after school?
- What games did you play?
- How did you watch your favourite TV shows or movies?
- What did you do during a train journey?
- How did you communicate with people living in other countries?
- How did you meet with your friends?

LOOKING FOR INFORMATION

If you have been able to ask these questions, you might have realized that before internet was invented, when you needed information about a certain subject you had to look for it in books! Nowadays, we have everything available to us with a simple click. Getting information on a topic is much quicker, and we can have access to a broader and more diverse net of data. But getting more information doesn't always mean getting better information. It can also give us a more superficial look at a subject. The average time we spend reading something on the internet is 40 seconds. Do we have time to understand and learn what we read in less than a minute?

The information found on the internet is not always factual. The so-called **fake news** is news that is false information and tries to make us believe that it's true. That's why it's increasingly important to learn to confirm the news we receive.

BEAVERS, CAT'S BEST FRIENDS

BEAVERS FROM THIS FARM CAN READ BOOKS.

BUILDING RELATIONSHIPS

Technology has made it possible for us to build relationships with people that are far away instantly.

But the same kind of technology that allowed us to stay in contact during the isolation of the COVID-19 pandemic, has been criticized because we are at risk of becoming isolated from our surroundings.

SPENDING TIME

Since electronic devices became popular, our time of leisure has changed. Lately there have been several studies to understand how children and teenagers spend their time. These studies show that the European youth spends between three and six hours online every day, and 26 percent of students are considered **extreme internet users** because they spend more than six hours a day online!

Which one of these situations do you like more?

Are there any that feel familiar to you?

Do any of them make you sad or worried?

HOW ADDICTIVE!

A lot of applications and games for smartphones and tablets get their revenue from how many users they have and how much time people spend on them. Therefore, they're created to make us spend as much time as possible using them and, that way, gather as much information as possible to sell it later. This business model is called the **data economy.**

Have you ever opened one of your favourite apps and, without even realizing, you have gotten stuck for a long time? Applications make sure to capture our attention. To do so, they use design tricks that keep us locked in.

SCIENCE SHOWS WHAT'S THE BEST AGE TO HAVE A DOG

Even though it's impossible to know what's the best age to have a dog because, in reality, it depends on a lot of factors…

YOU DON'T LIKE CHICKPEAS? YOU NEED TO READ THIS.

AMBIGUOUS TITLES

They generate curiosity and intrigue. We need to click and see their content! Now!

NOTIFICATIONS

The screen notifications demand our attention and encourage us to open the app.

GESTUAL DESIGN

The gestures that we must do to interact with smartphones and tablets are inspired by the idea of stroking a cat, so it's more pleasant to have the device in your hand.

64

REWARDS!

A very useful mechanism to modify our conduct is offering some kind of reward or positive reinforcement in exchange. This is especially effective if the reward is not predictable.

There are studies that show that if a mouse receives a variable amount of food every time a button is pressed, it will be more motivated to continue pressing the button than if it always receives the same amount.

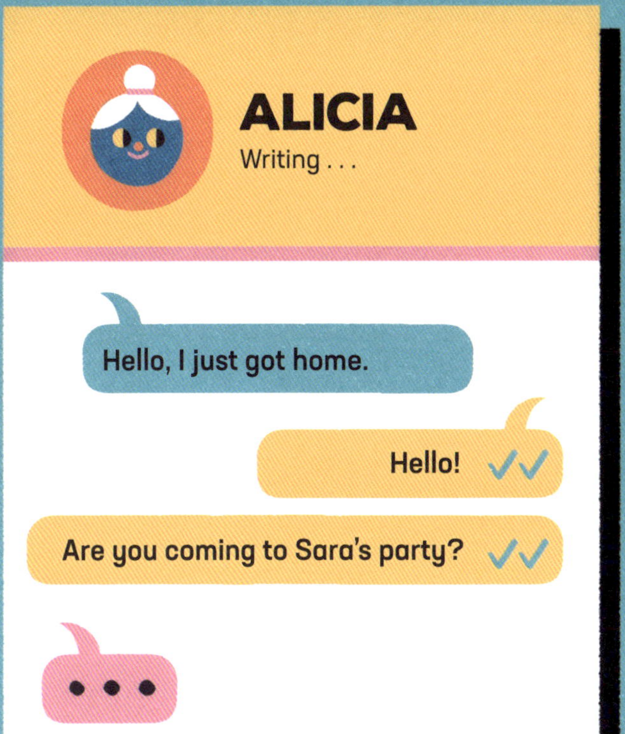

ALICIA
Writing . . .

Hello, I just got home.

Hello! ✓✓

Are you coming to Sara's party? ✓✓

Instant messaging apps can inform us if someone has received a message or not (and even if they have read it!), if someone is online, or if they are writing to us at that moment. What happens if we see that the person we just texted has seen the message but has not answered yet? And when we see they are writing?

NEXT EPISODE

Have you ever asked yourself why when we see a series on a streaming platform the next episode starts without us pressing play? It's been proved that this way people stay watching series for longer!

Sometimes those design tricks are almost imperceptible, but they can manage to change our behaviours. Now that we have given you a clue, would you be able to find them in your usual devices?

65

WHO CHANGES WHO?

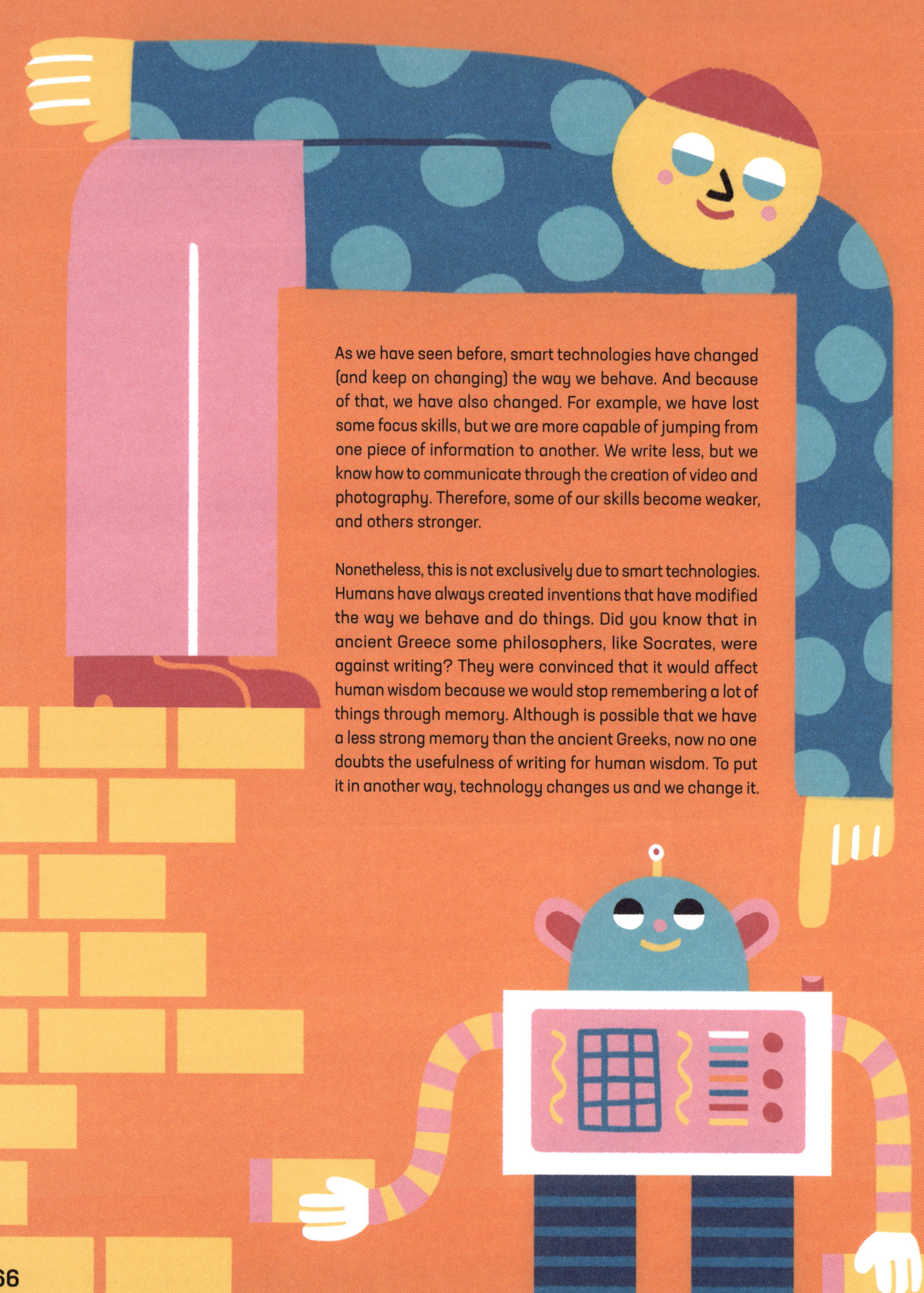

As we have seen before, smart technologies have changed (and keep on changing) the way we behave. And because of that, we have also changed. For example, we have lost some focus skills, but we are more capable of jumping from one piece of information to another. We write less, but we know how to communicate through the creation of video and photography. Therefore, some of our skills become weaker, and others stronger.

Nonetheless, this is not exclusively due to smart technologies. Humans have always created inventions that have modified the way we behave and do things. Did you know that in ancient Greece some philosophers, like Socrates, were against writing? They were convinced that it would affect human wisdom because we would stop remembering a lot of things through memory. Although is possible that we have a less strong memory than the ancient Greeks, now no one doubts the usefulness of writing for human wisdom. To put it in another way, technology changes us and we change it.

IMAGINE THE FUTURE!

And here we finish our trip to the world of smart machines. We have seen how they work, in which way they're used in different contexts, the challenges and possibilities offered, the way they are changing our habits, and deep down, also the way they're changing people. All these topics are very complex and bring up a wide variety of possible futures. Depending on the use and design we can create a fairer world or a more unfair one. It's our responsibility as users (and maybe even as possible future technology designers and creators) to be aware of it and try to try to do our part in the way we use technology and the way we imagine it.

And since we are talking about imagination, we can't forget that there are a lot of inventions that we consider common but had their first appearances in fictional stories. That's why it's so important to imagine the future! Would you like to join us?

How would we spend family time in the future? What kind of activities will we do during the weekends?

How will future children play and spend their days? Will they spend more time in front of a screen or will they be tired of them? Do you think that we will stop using screens in the future?

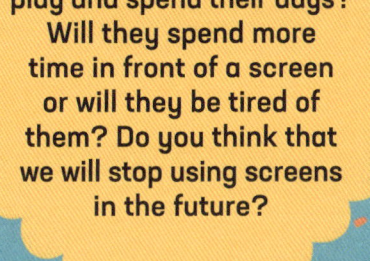

How would cities change if we spend increasingly less time outdoors? Will the current idea of what a city is stop making sense?

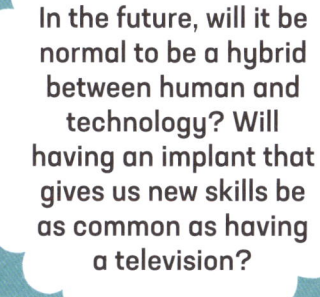

In the future, will it be normal to be a hybrid between human and technology? Will having an implant that gives us new skills be as common as having a television?

GLOSSARY

Algorithm Group of organized instructions used to resolve a problem or make a task. In the information field, these institutions are written in code for the computer to be able to interpret and execute orders.

Artificial intelligence Informatics field that has as an objective investigating and developing technologies capable of realising tasks considered human specific, per example, think and reason, make plans, draw own conclusions, connect things or give orders to move the body.

Automat Machine with a mechanism that allows it to move, specifically, imitating the figure and movement of a living thing, usually a human.

Data Facts, digits, images, sounds or any other kind of information about the world. They're always a limited representation of reality and the artificial intelligence results will depend on the given data.

Mental experiment Imaginative resource that consists in creating a hypothetical scene where we describe the expected actions and results from a situation. It's used to explain some side of reality or some reasoning.

Pattern or model Simplified version of reality in which we can find some of its main characteristics. To build patterns we need to analyze the received data.

Privacy Personal life field for everyone, developed in a reserved space. In the context of digital technologies, privacy refers to the right of the user to protect his own data online and decide which information is visible and to whom.

Programming Action of creating a series of instructions written in a specifical technical language, that provide the actions to be executed to the computer.

Stereotypes Pre-fixed idea about someone or something. They can interfere in the way you see and understand the world. Gender stereotypes, without going any further, can be reflected everywhere: toy's catalogues (pink things for girls, blue for boys, per example), in movies and cartoons (the prince is handsome and brave, the princess is beautiful and delicate), in advertisement (with ads in which only women deal with the house chores)…

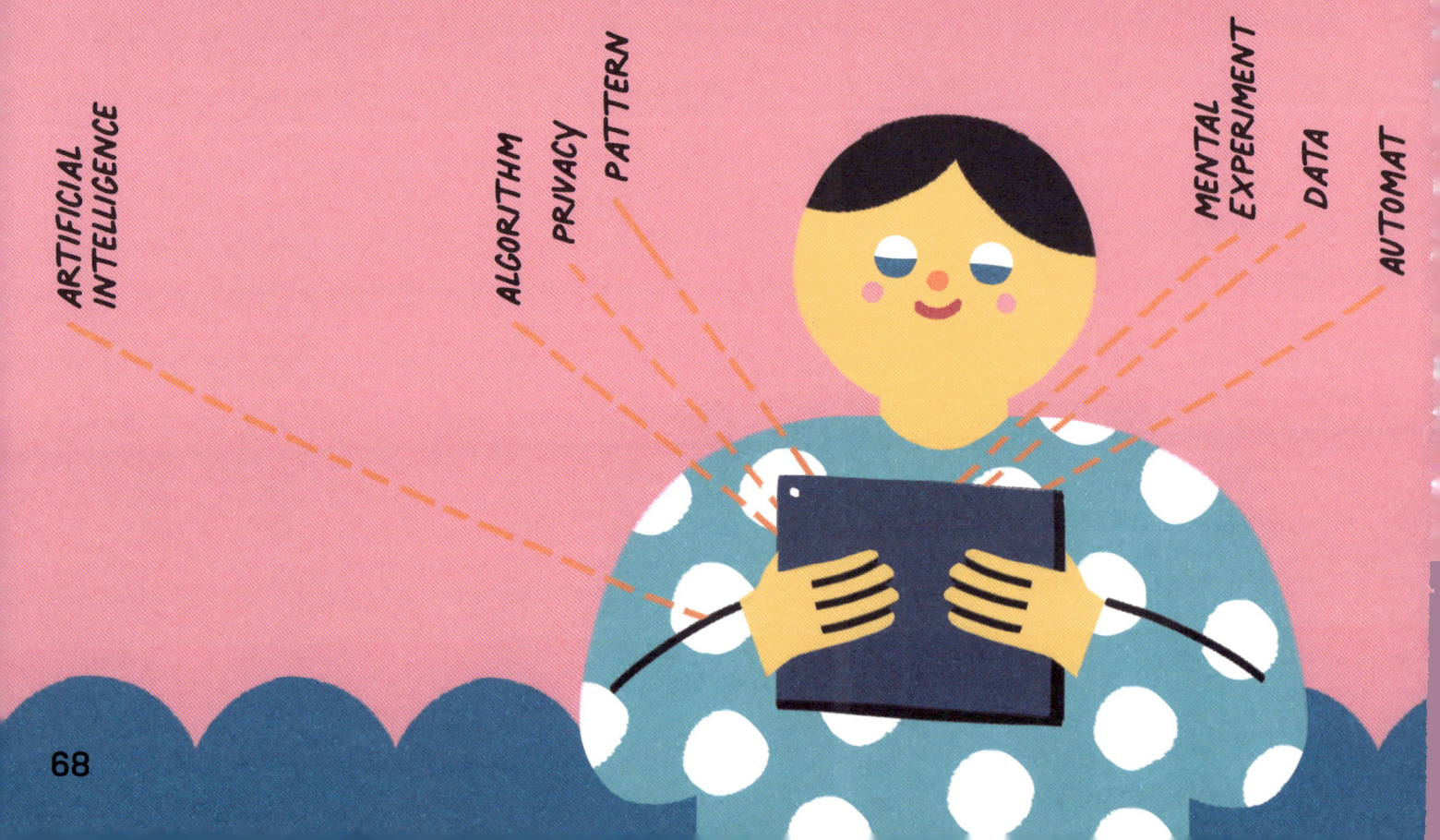

BIBLIOGRAPHY AND REFERENCES

SOCIOLOGICAL STUDIES
YOUNG PEOPLE AND THE USE OF NEW TECHNOLOGIES:

Burns, Tracey and Gottschalk, Francesca (ed), *Education in the Digital Age: Happy and healthy children,* OECD, Paris, France, 2020.

Common Sense Media: *The Common Sense Census: Media Use by Kids Age Zero to Eight.* Common Sense Media, 2017.

Hooft Graafland, Julie: *New technologies and 21st century children: Recent trends and outcomes.* OECD Education Working Papers, No. 179, OECD Publishing, Paris, 2018.

Livingstone, Sonia; Davidson, Julia; Bryce, Joanne; Batool, Saqba; Haughton, Ciaran; Nandi, Anulekha: *Children's online activities, risks and safety: A literature review by the UKCCIS Evidence Group.* LSE Consulting, London, 2017.

OECD: *A brave new world: Technology and education,* Trends Shaping Education Spotlights, n.o 15, OECD Publishing, Paris, 2018.

Smahel, David; Machackova, Hana; Mascheroni, Giovanna; Dedkova, Lenka; Staksrud, Elisabeth; Ólafsson, Kjartan; Livingstone, Sonia; Hasebrink, Uwe: *EU Kids Online 2020. Survey results from 19 countries.* EU Kids Online, 2020.

BOOKS AND ARTICLES TO REFLECT ON SMART TECHNOLOGIES

Cave, Stephen; Dihal, Kanta: *Ancient Dreams of Intelligent Machines: 3,000 years of Robots.* Nature, 559, 473-475, 26 July, 2018.

Cave, Stephen; Dihal, Kanta: *Hopes and Fears for Intelligent Machines in Fiction and Reality.* Nature Machine Intelligence, 1, 74-78, 2019.

Hannon, Charles: *Gender and status in voice user interfaces.* Interactions, xxiii, 34-37, June 2016.

Harari, Yuval Noah: *Homo Deus: A Brief History of Tomorrow.* Vintage Digital, 2016.

O'Neil, Cathy: *Weapons of Math Destruction: How Big Data Increases Inequality and Threatens Democracy.* Crown Publishing Group, 2016.

Royakkers, Lambèr; Timmer, Jelte; Kool, Linda; Van Est, Rinie: *Societal and Ethical Issues of Digitization.* Ethics and Information Technology, 20(2), 127-142, June 2018.

Torresen, Jim: *A review of future and ethical perspectives of robotics and AI.* Frontiers in Robotics and AI, 4:75, 15 January 2018.

Whittlestone, Jess; Nyrup, Rune; Alexandrova, Anna; Dihal, Kanta; Cave, Stephen: *Ethical and Societal Implications of Algorithms, Data, and Artificial Intelligence: A Roadmap for Research.* Nuffield Foundation, Londres, 2019.

VIDEOS AND ONLINE RESOURCES TO REFLECT ON SMART TECHNOLOGIES

Center for Humane Technologies. humanetech.com

Gender Shades. Mit Media Lab. gendershades.org

O'Neil, Cathy: *The era of blind faith in big data must end.* TED, April 2017.
ted.com/talks/cathy_o_neil_the_era_of_blind_faith_in_big_data_must_end?language=en

Pariser, Eli: *Beware online filter bubbles.* TED, March 2011.
ted.com/talks/eli_pariser_beware_online_filter_bubbles?language=en

NEWS ON MEDIA

Del Rio, Judith: *TikTok has as a rule not promoting videos of people that are ugly, poor, fat or with a disability*
La Vanguardia, 18 March, 2020.
lavanguardia.com/cribeo/cultura/20200318/474244004703/tik-tok-tiene-norma-promocionar-videos-gente-fea-pobre-gorda-dis- capacidad-redes-sociales-discriminacion.html

Jercich, Kat: *AI bias may worsen COVID-19 health disparities for people of color.* Healthcare IT News,
18 de agosto de 2020. healthcareitnews.com/news/ai-bias-may-worsen-covid-19-health- disparities-people-color

Rubio, Isabel: *Amazon gets rid of a recutting artificial intelligence because it was discriminating against women.*
The País, 12 October 2018.
elpais.com/tecnologia/2018/10/11/actuali- dad/1539278884_487716.html

Rubio, Isabel: *Employers of Amazon listen to people's conversations on Alexa on a daily basis.*
The País, 19 April 2019.
elpais.com/tecnologia/2019/04/11/actuali-dad/1554992401_521050.html

Rubio, Isabel: *Why it can be dangerous that an algorithm decides if you should be hired or give you a bank loan.*
The País, 23 November 2018.
elpais.com/tecnologia/2018/11/19/actuali-dad/1542630835_054987.html?rel=mas

Tsukayama, Hayley: *When your kid tries to say "Alexa" before "Mama."* The Washington Post, 21st November 2017.
washingtonpost.com/news/the-switch/wp/2017/11/21/when-your-kid-tries-to-say-alexa-before-mama/

Yujie, Xue: *Camera Above the Classroom.* Sixth Tone,
26 March 2019. sixthtone.com/news/1003759/camera-above-the-classroom